Indian Nations

THE SEMINOLES

by
E. Barrie Kavasch

General Editors
Herman J. Viola and Felix C. Lowe

A Rivilo Book

RSVP
RAINTREE
STECK-VAUGHN
PUBLISHERS
A Steck-Vaughn Company

Austin, Texas
www.steck-vaughn.com

*Dedicated to the Seminole People: their proud history,
their traditions, and their bright futures*

Sho-Naa-Bish (Thank you)

Published by Raintree Steck-Vaughn Publishers, an imprint of the
Steck-Vaughn Company

Developed for Steck-Vaughn Company
by Rivilo Books
Editor: David Jeffery
Photo Research: Paula Dailey
Design: Barbara Lisenby
Electronic Preparation: Curry Printing

Raintree Steck-Vaughn Publishers Staff
Publishing Director: Walter Kossmann
Editor: Kathy DeVico
Design Project Manager: Lyda Guz

Photo Credits: Peter Gallagher: cover; pp. 26, 28 right, 33, 39, 41; Lisa Ranallo Horse Capture: illustration, pp. 4, 7; Willard R. Culver/National Geographic Image Collection: pp. 8, 21 right, 28 left; Felix Lowe: pp. 9, 12; Otis Imboden/National Geographic Image Collection: pp. 10, 17, 20, 23, 24, 27, 29 left, 30, 31, 32, 36, 38; Smithsonian Anthropological Archives: pp. 11, 13, 15, 16, 18, 19, 29 right; E. Barrie Kavasch: pp. 21 left, 21 center, 22 bottom, 25 bottom, 37; Larry A. Lantz/First Mesa Inc.: p. 22 top; Archives and Manuscript Division of the Oklahoma Historical Society photo number 20615.12: p. 35; Annie Griffiths/National Geographic Image Collection: p. 25 top; Lyda Guz: p. 40.

We wish to thank Dr. Patricia Wickman and many others for their generous help.

Library of Congress Cataloging-in-Publication Data
Kavasch, E. Barrie.
    The Seminoles / by E. Barrie Kavasch; general editors, Herman J.
Viola and Felix C. Lowe.
        p.   cm. — (Indian nations)
    "A Rivilo book."
    Includes bibliographical references and index.
    Summary: Introduces the history, culture, and daily life of the Seminoles.
    ISBN 0-8172-5464-1
    1. Seminole Indians Juvenile literature.   [1. Seminole Indians.
    2. Indians of North America — Southern States.]   I. Viola, Herman J.
    II. Lowe, Felix C.   III. Title.   IV Series: Indian nations (Austin, Tex.)
    E99.S28K37   1999
    975.9'004973 — dc21

                                            99-28202
                                                CIP

Printed and bound in the United States of America
1 2 3 4 5 6 7 8 9 0 LB 03 02 01 00 99

Contents

"Panther Was First"... A Seminole Tribal Creation Story

In the earliest days, when the world was still brand-new, Breathmaker decided which animals would be the first to walk on the Earth. Breathmaker, who is the Grandfather of all things, had worked very hard creating the Earth. He had made so many exciting creatures to put there—reptiles, insects, spiders, and birds. While he was working, Panther, *Coo-wah-chobee (big cat)*, known as "crawls on four legs," would lie on the ground close beside him. Panther would rest his **regal** head on Breathmaker's foot. Breathmaker would often pause from his work and pet Panther, stroking his long, sleek back and tail. They had a special bond.

Because Breathmaker touched some creatures longer than others, more of his special powers flowed into them. Yet he made certain that all plants and animals possessed unique healing powers. Because each one had different abilities, they would always need one another. This is the way Breathmaker wove the web of life, making every living thing important to every other living thing.

Now Breathmaker began to breathe life into everything he had created. His powerful breath also created Wind, which is related to and touches everything in the world. As he worked

◄ *Breathmaker, the Grandfather of all things, gave life into everything he created.*

so carefully in those earliest days of time, Breathmaker said, "Panther, I want you to be the first to walk on the Earth. You have patience and strength. I feel your respect, and you will teach others about these qualities."

Breathmaker had worked very hard to make everything. He left nothing out. There was much more than we can see or know about today. The fresh, new Earth was covered with amazing plants of every sort. Wind blew around the world keeping things dancing and in touch with Breathmaker's great energies. Breathmaker said to Wind, "You will embrace everything on the Earth, giving them new energy and life. Without you stirring the air we breathe, things will die."

Finally Breathmaker put all of the animals into a huge shell and placed the shell upon the Earth beside a great palm tree. He asked the animals to rest and talk together—to get to know each other—before they went out on their separate ways to live free in the world.

Time passed slowly. All of the two-legged and four-legged creatures mingled with the six-legged and eight-legged creatures, and the millipedes squirmed over everyone. The feathered and finned and scaled and furred beings all visited and talked together. The slimy and naked and hard-shelled beings wiggled and crawled around, speaking among themselves. Much time passed. Wind kept blowing across this sacred gathering of animals and rushing about through the great trees and other plants.

Occasionally one of the animals would walk close to the edge of the giant shell, but no one ventured out. They remembered what Breathmaker had said. Several times Turtle almost slipped over the edge, but Alligator caught him and brought him back into the group.

Finally, the animals had waited long enough and began to fidget. They were eager to be free and go to their new homes. Wind blew around them, bringing strange new fragrances. Panther walked to the edge of the giant shell. Ever patient, he reminded all the animals of their special qualities. As Wind blew stronger, Panther jumped over the edge of the giant shell and loped off through the Everglades.

Wind was blowing everywhere. Birds flew out chirping happily, followed by all of the insects that could fly. Next emerged Deer and Bear. They were followed by Frog, Otter, Alligator, and Snake. Each one breathed in Wind, which gave them added energy for their journeys.

Many thousands of creatures emerged at that time. All went off to seek their places in the world. Breathmaker watched over everything with special interest. He allowed everything to happen in its own natural time. And it is still this way today.

Origins

In the Seminole creation story, Breathmaker gave each animal and plant healing powers along with its unique qualities of beauty, strength, patience, or cunning. Breathmaker also gave the Seminole people an understanding of these powers. Qualities of certain animals are associated with the different

The Wheel of Life here is explained by Josie Billie, an elder, who was a living treasure of Seminole knowledge.

clans or family groups within the Seminole tribe. Panther Clan people, for example, became known for protecting the people and for preparing healing medicines.

Bird was also chosen as a clan leader. The ability to fly makes Bird an overseer of the order of things. Many people believe that birds can fly so high that they are closer to the Creator than other animals and humans. For this reason, bird feathers are placed in some ceremonial objects.

The Wind Clan also takes leadership roles. Wind is the brother of Panther and all living things. Wind is there beside Panther whenever medicines are being made and celebrations are being planned. Wind must always stir things up. Wind adds more creative energy to everything.

Knowledge about the healing qualities of plants is preserved by the **elders** and traditional medicine men of the Seminole tribe. They keep the sacred medicine bundles and arrange their blessing during the annual **Green Corn Ceremony.**

James E. Billie, the Seminole Tribal Chairman, describes this event: "Today, among the Seminoles and other Indian people, there are ceremonies on the occasion of the greening of the earth. At these ceremonies, you can see the Panther, with brother Wind, mixing the medicines for all people to use."

Among the Seminoles, as among other American Indians, elders are known as "living treasures" of tribal history, traditional ways, and knowledge of healing. The elders use storytelling to keep traditions vivid in the present.

"Alligator and Rabbit Visit"... A Lesson in Trust

Rabbit was always little and furry, but he was loud and sassy in earlier times and usually up to some mischief. Among the smaller animals and birds, Rabbit was always trying to show off. Many Seminole stories recall how Rabbit told lies and bothered other animals. Nevertheless, Rabbit and big Alligator were friends.

Back in those earliest times, there was only one language, and all the animals could understand each other. Rabbit and Alligator used to enjoy visiting and talking together. Rabbit was always testing Alligator, who was usually in a peaceful, lazy mood. Alligator loved to lay about in the hot sun. Rabbit was usually bored and looking for mischief.

Rabbit came hopping along one day, showing off, studying his reflection near the water's edge. Rabbit asked Alligator to give him swimming lessons in the Big Cypress Swamp, and Alligator agreed. But it was a hot, lazy day, and big Alligator soon fell asleep in the sun.

One time before, Rabbit had tricked big Alligator into telling where his weak spots were and how he might be hurt. Now while Alligator basked and slept in the hot sun,

Alligator likes to fall asleep in the warm sun.

9

Rabbit took a big stick and smacked him hard between the eyes and on his back. Wham! Wham! This hurt Alligator.

But friendship and trust were hurt, too. And since that long-ago time, big Alligator will eat little Rabbit and any of his relatives if he can catch them! So Rabbit is no longer loud and sassy but quiet and shy.

Storytelling

Storytelling is one of the ways the Seminole people keep their **traditions** alive. Wherever stories are told, they usually reflect the beliefs and geography of the storytellers. Seminole stories are just a little different from the stories of their Creek and Cherokee neighbors. However, they are very different from the stories of other Indian tribes.

Rabbit is not bossy any more but quiet and shy.

Picture evenings spent sitting around a smoky fire in the deep South. A smoky fire is necessary to keep the mosquitoes and other bugs away. Here Seminole children enjoy listening to the stories elders tell about "how things got to be this way."

These old Seminole stories are full of characters like Rabbit, Alligator, Squirrel, Eagle, and many more. Storytellers use these characters to weave life's lessons together with humor. The jokes poke fun at the listeners yet illuminate values they care about at the same time. Tricksters, like Rabbit, often teach by misbehaving. Creatures will sometimes take advantage of one another just as people do. Rabbit also shows how "the little guy" can sometimes win against great odds.

Key Historical Events

The Seminole creation story stretches back to the beginning of time. **Ancestors** of the Seminole Indians have lived in the Southeast for more than 10,000 years. **Archaeology** is the recovery and study of the remains of the way humans lived long ago. Archaeologists have discovered finely made stone spear points and arrowheads in Florida that are more than 4,000 years old. In addition to tools, there is evidence of ancient roads, canals, and burial mounds that were created by these stone age people. Beautiful objects made by prehistoric Indian people are displayed in some of Florida's museums.

The Calusa Indians, who had established an empire across southern Florida, carved many beautiful objects from bone and wood like this kneeling cat found at Key Marco, Florida.

The Environment

Florida has long been "Indian Country." The sun-drenched **peninsula** spreads over 60,000 square miles (155,400 sq km) of flat **semitropical** lowlands. All is bordered by more than 8,000 miles (12,900 km) of coastline. Beaches dot the Atlantic and Gulf of Mexico coasts. Ancestors of the Seminoles chose this land, and it provided for all of their needs.

Thousands of islands are sanctuaries for nesting birds. Sea turtles come ashore to lay their eggs. **Manatees**, otters, and alligators swim in rivers along with countless frogs, fish, and crawfish. Forests and brush between broad **savannas** are home to panthers, deer, and raccoons. Florida's first people found plenty to eat in every season. The trick was knowing how to catch it.

11

The Everglades are rich in fresh water, islands, trees, animals, fish, and plants which are used as medicine.

The **Everglades** cover more than 4,000 square miles (10,360 sq km) of south-central Florida with broad marshlands filled with tropical life. Tall cypress trees, palms, and thick mangrove swamps are draped with gray-green patches of Spanish moss. These resources provided the Indians with dugout canoes, food, and clothing. Climbing vines and distinctive medicine plants flourish there. Wood storks, ibis, and herons stalk various fish, frogs, and crawfish in shallow waters.

Seminole Ancestors

The Calusa Indians were perhaps the first to live in southwestern Florida. Some other tribes were the Ocali, Potano, and Tequesta Indians. These were distant ancestors of the Seminoles. These Indians lived in their own distinct settlements and traded with one another. They traveled the shallow rivers and swamps by dugout canoe. They fished and trapped wild food in inland waterways. Over time, members of those tribes mixed together naturally through friendships and marriages.

The Southeast was also the homeland of the Timucua, Guale, and Apalachicola Indians. Hitchiti and Eufaula Indians also made encampments in southeastern regions. These Indian people were also distant relatives of the Seminole.

North of Florida, in what is now Alabama and Georgia, lived other native peoples. Some were farmers, while others were fishermen and hunters. Those tribes included the Maskókî, Yuchi, and Yamassees. The Indians whom the English called "Creeks" commonly built their villages on the banks of southern streams.

The First Explorers

Early European explorations brought change. The Spanish explorer Juan Ponce de León named Florida in 1513 and claimed it for Spain. Several centuries of Spanish domination and rule followed. The fierce opposition of the Native peoples prevented the Spaniards from controlling the wealth of Florida, which lay in its people and its plant and animal life.

To hunt and fish, Seminole men poled dugout canoes through marshlands of south-central Florida.

Changing Settlements

Cultural conflict has colored much of Florida's history. Pressure from waves of land-hungry white settlers forced many Indians to move away from their homelands. Various Maskókî tribes shifted southward from Georgia and Alabama in the early 1700s. The Yamassee also rose up against English planters over trading in the South Carolina area, resulting in further migration of these Indians into northern Florida in 1715.

These southern Indians joined the natives in the Spanish territories of Florida. They were the ancestors of the people who became known as Seminoles.

The Seminoles Emerge

The term Seminole comes from the Indian term for them, *yat' siminóli,* which means "free people." The term may also be traced to the Spanish *cimarrón,* which means "wild" (free) or "unconquered." The Seminoles share languages and many traditions with their Maskókî ("Creek") relatives.

In 1763 Britain received Florida from Spain in exchange for Cuba. The English held it until their defeat in the American Revolution. The Treaty of Paris returned Florida to Spanish rule in 1783, but continuing quarrels between European powers added to Seminole distrust of governing powers.

Seminole Wars

Still later, some Florida Seminoles supported Britain or Spain against the United States in the devastating War of 1812. Even after it lost the war, Britain encouraged Indian raids north into Georgia. These hostilities led to the First Seminole War in 1817 and 1818. General Andrew Jackson led an army of 3,000 Americans into Spanish Florida. The army burned Seminole villages and destroyed crops. Troops looked for escaped slaves and burned settlements and farms of black families. Most of the Seminole and Miccosukee Indians and their black allies avoided capture by moving deeper into the Florida interior. These Indian allies were skilled fighters who held out against the Army for many years.

Among them was the young **mixed-blood** Osceola. He was born a Maskókî in what is now Alabama. In 1814, to escape American troops who served under Andrew Jackson, Osceola and his mother fled to Florida. They joined their relatives, the Seminoles, and Osceola emerged as a valiant, colorful freedom fighter.

In 1818, after the first Seminole War, the United States made a demand of Spain: "Control the Seminoles, or give Florida to us." A year later, Spain did give Florida to the United States. In exchange,

In the 1830s Osceola led the Seminoles in struggles with U.S. officials, only to die in prison.

the United States gave up claims to Texas and paid Spain's debts to U.S. citizens. Florida became a Territory of the United States in 1821.

General Andrew Jackson became president in 1829. In 1830 he signed into law the Indian Removal Act, which allowed the U.S. government to remove Indians from their lands in the East to areas west of the Mississippi River. The removal treaties were supposed to be voluntary. However, many tribal leaders were misled into signing them. Armed settlers also began to occupy Indian lands. The Florida Seminole and Miccosukee Indians simply moved deeper into the wild interior regions. They tried to survive against the government's pressures.

More treaties and deceptions led to the outbreak of the Second Seminole War in December 1835. Osceola participated in several successful Seminole attacks. More and more soldiers were sent to Florida, and the war dragged on for two years. Then, tired of war, Osceola and some of his Seminole warriors agreed to meet with a detachment of soldiers. They would talk of peace—but not surrender. The Seminoles came bearing a white flag of truce. But the soldiers did not honor the flag or the truce and captured them. Osceola was put in prison and in 1838 died at age 34 while suffering from a throat infection. The long, costly **guerrilla** campaign was over. It was the most expensive Indian war fought by the U.S., and many people had been killed on both sides.

Eventually more than 3,400 Seminoles were captured and deported in various groups to Indian Territory in present-day Oklahoma. Harsh conditions and forced marches caused many to die. By the spring of 1842, the government reported a total of 2,833 "Seminoles and Negroes" living in Oklahoma.

People of the Everglades

Scattered by years of fighting, about 500 Seminoles and Miccosukees remaining in Florida moved deeper into the Big Cypress Swamp and the Everglades. They continued to avoid white settlers for years, until the Third Seminole War began in 1855.

Chief Billy Bowlegs rallied his people during the Third Seminole War in the 1850s.

The Florida militia and some federal troops attacked Seminole settlements in the Big Cypress Swamp. This final attempt to drive the Seminoles out of Florida was not successful. However, more Seminoles were killed, and another 200 were deported west to Indian Territory.

To survive attack, Seminoles built homes like these deep in the Big Cypress Swamp well away from white settlements.

Many Seminole people try to have nothing to do with the U.S. government today, because they recall the long history of persecution and war. Today the Seminole people remain in control of their own destiny.

Way of Life

Clans

The Seminoles are made up of special **clans**. Each newborn Seminole baby is a member of his or her Seminole mother's clan. This is their traditional larger family unit of relatives. When they grow up, they are supposed to marry a person of another clan.

There are eight Seminole clans in Florida today. They are called the Panther, Bear, Otter, Deer, Bird, Snake, Bigtown, and Wind clans. The clans might be further divided by animal size. Some Panther Clan members, for example, may be Big Panther (tiger) or Little Panther (bobcat). Bird Clan members can be either Big Bird or Little Bird.

There were once many more Seminole clans in Florida. Some clans have died out, and others have moved to Oklahoma, where they continue to flourish. The largest clan in the Seminole Tribe of Florida today is the Panther Clan.

Seminole clans preserve tribal customs and weave special meanings from past history into present life. The animal names of the clans, for example, offer rich associations with Seminole stories. Symbols of these animals might appear in arts and crafts. The Bigtown Clan symbol is usually a frog or toad. The Wind Clan symbol often pictures a person blowing. Both the wind and the

Tom Tiger and his family in the late 1800s. From birth, Seminoles are members of one of eight clans.

18

breath are important elements in Seminole tradition. Medicine men would often blow on or into medicines with a special blowpipe, or bubbling pipe, to "energize" the healing potentials of the herbs.

Housing

During the historic period, the Florida Seminoles lived in camps built on high ground surrounded by fertile gardens. The women elders managed the camp, and the large, extended families shared the work, especially the hunting and gathering jobs. A camp included several large **chickees** covering wooden platforms where people slept, and one large cooking chickee, with an earthen floor, where everyone cooked and ate together. Chickees are distinctive Seminole houses, ideal for Florida, with palmetto thatched roofs and open sides, built around a sturdy wooden frame.

People usually traveled from camp to camp in long dugout canoes carved from bald cypress logs. Bald cypress "knees" (the knobby rootlike parts that stick up out of the water) were hollowed out and covered with buckskin to make ceremonial drums.

Seminole camps included "chickees," open structures used for eating or for sleeping.

Today the Seminole Tribe Housing Authority looks after modern housing needs for Florida tribal members. Seminole families can **lease** one and one-half acres of land and receive an affordable mortgage to build a house. The U.S. Department of Housing and Urban Development provides some money to **subsidize** tribal housing. Early CBS (cement block structure) houses were built on several **reservations**. These houses were able to withstand the destructive hurricanes that occasionally pound southern Florida. Many families also maintain open-air chickees beside their modern homes.

Clothing

The creativity of the Seminoles is often celebrated in their famous patchwork. In this craft, brightly colored cotton cloth is carefully cut into small shapes, then sewn back together in complex patterns. The **patchwork** fabric is then used to make jackets, vests, blouses, and skirts. Garments may be further decorated with solid color bands or **rickrack**. Seminole men, women, and children wear their distinctive clothing, both old-style and modern, with pride.

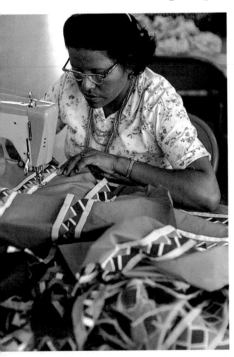
Machine sewing helps speed creation of colorful fabrics, dresses, and shirts.

Interestingly, however, Seminole patchwork is not an ancient tradition. Traders introduced European cloth to Native Americans about 400 years ago. The ancestors of the Seminoles, both men and women, wore Spanish moss or buckskin clothes. Deerskin and other animal hides were plentiful then, and buckskin clothing is very durable (many white settlers favored it in the colonial period).

Seminole women readily accepted the bright calicos, ribbons, and shawls brought in through trade. They made cotton jackets, shirts, and long skirts following the styles of European clothes. Once sewing machines became available in the late 1800s, Seminole clothing became more and more elaborate and distinctive. Women pieced together colorful scraps or material leftover from other clothes they had made for their families. Fine patchwork was alternated with bands of plain cotton or calico fabric. In this way the beautiful style of Seminole patchwork developed.

The Seminoles have always been very particular about their appearance. Their sense of style for clothing and hair has made them famous and widely photographed. Beaded sashes and belts made of fingerwoven wool were and still are worn by Seminole men with their traditional clothing. Hairstyles, too, have been remarkable. Traditional Seminole men often wore colorful turbans wound around their heads to protect their hair and to show their social status. Leaders and medicine men, especially, wore handsome turbans adorned with **egret** feather plumes. Earlier in the 20th century, Seminole women and girls would brush their long black hair up toward their foreheads. They would then fasten it over **black boards** (or hair forms), and secure it with dark hairnets. Few Seminole women still wear their hair this way.

Fine patchwork garments (left), colorful attire for men (below), and heavy beaded necklaces and black board hairstyles (right) have been traditional favorites worn on special occasions.

Arts and Crafts

Fine patchwork sewing is the most famous Seminole art. Some say this Seminole piecing is another language, expressing proud traditions in colors and symbols. Talented seamstresses sew detailed zigzags to represent lightning and rain.

Seminole-style clothing is made for sale and is often seen at Indian **powwows**, fairs, and rodeos. Some rock stars, movie stars, and presidents wear stunning Seminole vests and jackets. Patchwork designs also are used to create aprons, potholders, table linens, and countless other sale items. Pretty palmetto fiber and cloth dolls dressed in traditional clothes and hairstyles are also favorites.

Dolls made from palmetto fiber are dressed in costume.

Many Seminole men and boys enjoy carving wooden items for home use and the tourist trade. Large spoons or ladles are always in demand. They also carve various simple toys to challenge young minds and fingers. Toy dugout canoes are made for children to play with.

Women weave pine needle or sweet grass baskets in classic shapes. Seminole children often weave simple basket coils around palmetto fiber centers.

Seminole arts and crafts are products of native enterprise and the tribe's history and unique Florida environment. The best examples are highly prized by collectors.

Maggie Osceola's fingers fly as she makes beautiful baskets and bowls from natural fibers such as palmetto.

Religion, Traditions, and Ceremonies

Seminole traditions are their most time-honored beliefs and practices that have been carried on through generations. Many aspects of Seminole life are celebrated, and the most special is the sacred Green Corn Ceremony. This annual four-day celebration requires several days of advance preparation. It is usually held in the early summer at a private location. No outsiders are permitted to attend. A day of fasting and purification is followed by the Feast of Green Corn. Usually only Seminole men participate in the rituals of fasting and purification, because women are considered to be purified already.

The Green Corn Ceremony is the traditional renewal of the whole tribe. The medicine bundles are opened and displayed for 24 hours, while the medicine man starts a new fire using the special flint kept in the bundle. An all-night vigil is held by the medicine man and his assistants, and during this time the medicines are renewed. Many believe that if the Green Corn Ceremony were not performed regularly every year, the medicine would lose its powers, and the tribe would die.

During the four-day Green Corn Ceremony in summer, Oklahoma Seminoles join in the spirited "Stomp Dance."

The traditional game of stickball requires great skill. Men use two webbed cypress sticks, or rackets, to hold the ball, while women players may use their hands.

Community Activities

Tribal renewal is the main reason for ceremonies, but various community and social events also encourage everyone to have a good time. Tribal leaders gather for meetings to discuss political matters, to settle disputes, and to promote forgiveness. Social dances and games are also popular. Stickball is an ancient game much like today's field hockey. Players use two long-handled wooden rackets, in which a small deerskin ball is caught and carried or hurled toward the goal. In earlier days each team would represent a different town in vigorous matches that tested the players' athletic skill and endurance. Although stickball has a ceremonial function, it is often a social event with boys competing against girls.

Celebrating Life

While the Green Corn traditions remain private and personal, the Seminoles share many tribal events publicly, and people attend these events from all over the world. A series of annual powwows, fairs, and rodeos are scheduled throughout "Seminole Country" in both Florida and Oklahoma. Visitors are welcomed, entertained, fed, and treated with respect. Seminole hospitality is legendary!

Seminole young people dress in Plains Indian style for a powwow in Oklahoma.

Powwows and fairs are filled with great energy and excitement, as three and four generations of Seminoles gather to show off their finest clothing, share their best foods, and dance in the many dance competitions. Indians from all across the Americas come to these Seminole events. It is not unusual to see the Aztec Fire Dancers performing as featured guests, along with Indian drum groups representing tribes from Canada to New Mexico. Jingle Dress Dancers, Grass Dancers, and Fancy Dancers usually start practicing early to develop their athletic form and perfect their dance steps to take part in these powwows.

Foods

While attending a Seminole powwow, you might get deep-fried 'gator nuggets to eat with your Seminole pumpkin frybread or Indian taco salad. They are best enjoyed with a delicious Seminole smoothie, which is a frothy, ice-cold citrus drink. (The recipe is on page 40.) Turkey sausages and venison (deer) sausages are served with spicy rice and beans. Another meal consists of the classic *sofkee,* a light corn gruel or beverage, served hot.

A cook at a Seminole powwow dishes up sausages to eat with frybread.

In Seminole tradition, the alligator, turkey, and rabbit were considered sacred animals. Certain rules and practices had to be followed when killing and eating them. Time and changing economic patterns have modified those beliefs.

Frogs, crayfish, and turtles are also favorite foods for many people, especially in the South. Traditionally, Seminole "froggers" set up temporary camps along shallow inland waterways to catch these creatures. Some still trap frogs in that way and sell their catch to neighboring families and nearby restaurants.

Seminole medicine woman, Suzie Billie, gathers herbs.

Medicines

Traditional Seminole medicine has a valuable role in modern life. Seminole medicine people (sometimes called **shamans**) knew the healing powers of **herbs** and plants. Chief James Billie sings a popular ballad about one such herbalist, a famous medicine man named Josie Billie. He was completely at home in the cypress swamps and knew how to use many wild plants. Seminole medicine people who today continue to use plants and herbs for healing are greatly respected.

Some doctors and scientists recognize the many virtues of Seminole medicines made from plants. They use saw palmetto to treat prostate problems and cancers. The cabbage palm fern provides remedies for asthma and stomach problems. Buttonwood provides an **astringent** to cure skin diseases. Gumbo limbo, a subtropical tree, is used to make a medicinal antiseptic, and extracts from hibiscus, a flowering bush, treats various eye problems and **hypertension**. Seminole herbalism continues to enrich our lives.

Christianity

Missionaries from various Christian churches have long been active among some of the Seminole groups. Many have made friends with the Seminole people. The Episcopalian and Baptist faiths were most active within the native camps and communities.

By the mid-1900s, a few Seminole people accepted some Christian beliefs. When Josie Billie, a respected medicine man or shaman, converted to Christianity, many others were moved to follow. Still, many Seminole people hold sacred their time-honored traditions. Most Seminole people participate in tribal gatherings and ceremonies whenever they can.

After the 1950s some Seminole men were ordained as Baptist ministers and gathered faithful followings. Churches have been built on the reservations and today are supported by many families.

Children learn traditional beliefs as well as the A-B-Cs of schoolwork.

Family Life

Traditional Seminole family life was centered around work. Children learned the skills and attitudes they would need in life by working with their parents and relatives, especially the folks in their mothers' clans. Work tasks and chores in Seminole camps and settlements depended on the season. Gardening, farming, hunting, and fishing were necessary for most families.

Hunting was a good example of the way Seminole families worked together. The men hunted the game, including deer, rabbit, squirrel, raccoon, wild turkey, duck, and geese. Men

dressed the meat and women prepared it. Women and young children often preserved the valuable hides, skins, and feathers for later use. These time-consuming tasks were best shared with families and relatives. Everyone contributed to the survival of the clan.

Henry John Billie (in hat), the last of the Seminole dugout canoe makers, stands next to his latest project (right). Chief James E. Billie leans on the newly finished work. Another expert works on curing a buckskin (above).

Roles of Parents and Relatives

Fathers and uncles taught the boys how to hunt and fish and helped them develop their skills through games. Keen marksmanship and good hand-eye coordination were highly valued skills. Young boys were given small bows and arrows and sometimes small spears to throw at rolling rings or targets. Blowguns and darts were also weapons of choice for hunting small game animals and birds in the lush Florida environment. Many hours of training and target practice were necessary before a boy ever went hunting.

Women taught the older girls and all young children the vital tasks of food gathering and cooking. Seminole foods were often prepared in communal groups. The talk was cheerful, and everyone enjoyed working together. Young girls grew up within the circle of clan relatives sharing their various skills and stories. Each girl's abilities were cultivated to find what she could do best.

Many years ago a family (right) prepared a meal in the shade of a "chickee," and a more modern woman (below) watches her grandchildren at Bass Day, a fishing festival.

Games and Sports

Games like stickball and lacrosse had their origins in religious ritual. Yet they also tested young people's coordination, speed, and endurance. Likewise, through various forms of tribal dancing, Seminole children learned to move quickly and gracefully. These activities also developed a sense of teamwork among those who took part. Many traditional games were practiced for life's more serious needs. For example, hunting skills, such as stalking and tracking, grew out of watching the animals. Those skills are still important because hunting continues to be a preferred source of food in some areas on the reservations. As Seminole children grow older, their games and activities support their roles in family, school, and community.

Games teach teamwork, and a young athlete is doing his part with a mighty swing at a softball.

New Traditions

In some ways, modern Seminole families live very different-ly from their ancestors. Family groups are smaller and do not always live near their clan relatives or tribal base. Some families have moved to cities for greater opportunities in work and education. Many more Seminoles are attending college and then landing well-paid jobs throughout the United States. When lifestyles change, new traditions evolve to suit them.

When Jenny Osceola (left) and Jenny Micco graduated from high school in the late 1960s, few went on to college. Now, many do.

Seminole cowboys have existed since the Maskókî first received cattle from the Spanish in the 17th century. Rodeo riding and roping events are relatively recent and command much attention among Seminole young people today. Cattle projects are important activities for 4-H youth groups, espe-cially on the Brighton and Big Cypress reservations in Florida.

Tribal Life

The Seminole people have been treated harshly in the past, yet they have regrouped and flourished. They have much to teach us about survival, pride, and renewal. As we visit with them and listen to their voices, we gain new respect for their distinctive history.

Seminole people pay state and federal taxes just like every U.S. citizen. Both the chairman of the Tribal Council and the president of the Seminole Tribe of Florida are elected by popular vote and serve four-year terms. Major tribal priorities are programs focused on health, education, and housing. These are vital areas, central to improving the lives of everyone in the tribe. Additional economic programs are managed by the tribe for its members.

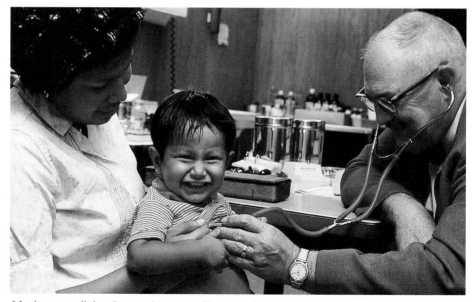

Modern medicine is used to treat illness, although some Seminoles also use the old natural medicines.

Seminole Tribe of Florida

The Florida Seminoles have endured and prospered despite their history of persecution. By the early 1900s, Congress had acted to stop Florida settlers from moving onto Indian lands. Brighton Reservation was established for the Cow Creek band of the Seminoles. Big Cypress Reservation was set aside for the Miccosukee branch of the Seminoles, and the Hollywood (Dania) Reservation (near Ft. Lauderdale) was established for the entire tribe. In 1957 the Seminole Tribe of Florida was formed, and members elected a chairman, a president, and a leadership council.

The headquarters building of the Seminole Tribe of Florida is located in Hollywood, Florida, and is modern in every way.

The Florida Seminoles maintain five separate reservations today with more land at Immokalee and Tampa. Almost 2,000 tribal members live in their reservation communities and manage more than 90,000 acres (36,400 ha). Tribal bingo and casino operations have enabled the Seminoles to prosper and grow. Health, education, and business opportunities continue to increase. Florida Seminoles are financially one of the most independent tribes in America today.

Tribal libraries and schools are flourishing in Florida. The "crown jewel" of Seminole tribal education is the beautiful Ahfachkee Indian School at Big Cypress Reservation. *Ahfachkee* means "happy" in the Miccosukee language. It educates Seminole students from kindergarten through high school. The Ahfachkee school is paid for in part by the U.S. **Bureau of Indian Affairs** and in part by the Seminole Tribe of Florida. Other resources include preschool and adult education classes, job training, and child care programs.

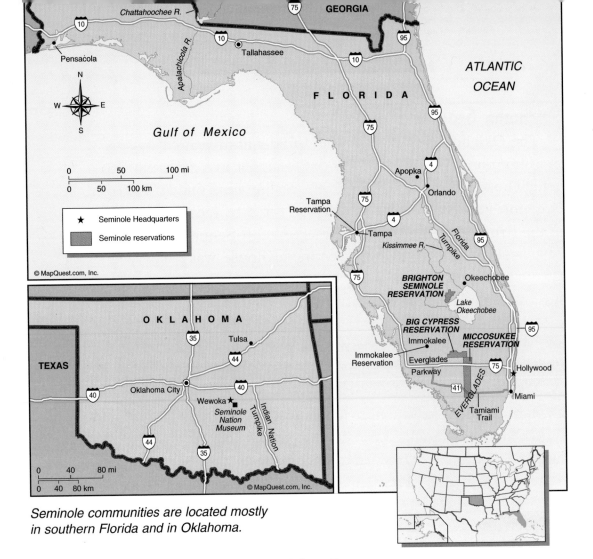

Seminole communities are located mostly in southern Florida and in Oklahoma.

Miccosukee Tribe of Florida

The Miccosukee Tribe of Florida was established in 1961 and has an elected chairman and leadership council. Many are referred to as "The Trail Indians" because of their homes, businesses, and tourist attractions along the Tamiami Trail. This is a highway that cuts across the southern width of the Florida peninsula through the Everglades. The Miccosukee Reservation is located in the Everglades and is divided by the Everglades Parkway, known as "Alligator Alley."

Another group of Seminoles are known as "Independents." They wish to remain free of any tribal authority.

Oklahoma Seminoles

The Oklahoma Seminoles spent many hard years trying to survive among some of their historic enemies in a difficult new land. The weather, foods, and ways of life were very different from their eastern homeland. They worked to reconfirm their tribal structure and, in 1868, formed the Seminole Nation in Wewoka, Oklahoma. A new council house was built, and the Seminole government elected a principal chief, a second chief, and a 42-member council. The Seminole Lighthorsemen (mounted police) enforced their laws, and though they were only a small force, gained a reputation for honesty, ability, and courage.

Exploration for natural gas and oil began in 1902 in Oklahoma, and the Greater Seminole Oil Field near Wewoka was opened in 1923. Economic resources increased, as did Seminole population. Oklahoma Seminoles have devoted a great deal of time and resources to education and health care.

The Seminole Lighthorsemen, seen here in a 1904 photo, enforced the laws of the Seminole Nation in Oklahoma with bravery and integrity.

Contemporary Seminole Life

Cowboys

Cattle are big business in the South, and in Florida many of the cowboys are Indians. Seminoles are award-winning ropers, riders, and successful cattle ranchers. Some ranchers even herd their cows and horses by helicopter.

The Seminole tribe's modern cattle program began in 1926. They got their livestock from the drought-starved Apache Indian herds in the Southwest. Selective breeding, careful farming and ranching practices, and good business management have enabled Seminole herds to grow.

The Seminole Tribe is celebrated as the third largest beef producer in Florida. Each August the Annual Seminole Tribe of Florida Cattle Drive and Sale is held. All of the cowboys help each other round up the cattle from the many pastures on the reservations. Almost 3,000 calves were sold after the 1997 roundup. In recent years many fine calves have been sold at **auctions** conducted through satellite communications hookups and have been shipped to the West. Florida Seminoles also ranch bison (buffalo), hogs, and other animals.

Beef cattle are important to Florida, and Seminole ranchers have made great progress in raising fine herds.

Alligators

Alligators, which figure in so many Seminole stories and traditions, are also big business in Florida today. Once endangered by overhunting, alligators have made a big comeback and are thriving again. These amazing reptiles are a source of fine food, and their tanned hides make beautiful, costly shoes and leather goods. Alligators are raised on farms in order to meet the growing demands.

Alligator wrestling is a classic demonstration of Seminole courage and showmanship. The elders say the reason Seminole people have always "messed with" alligators and teased them is precisely because they are dangerous! Yet alligator wrestling as a dynamic sport probably began in the 1920s as a tourist attraction designed to draw visitors to Florida. It still does!

Today's Seminole alligator and snapping turtle wrestlers are athletes, entertainers, and teachers all rolled into one. Calm and professional, they present programs filled with facts and respect for these ancient reptiles and their natural environment. The programs educate growing audiences about the habits of dangerous animals and how to be careful when near them. Many Seminole showmen are careful not to wrestle any one alligator or snapping turtle too much—so as not to break its spirit.

Alligator wrestling is a popular test of skill and draws crowds from all over the country.

A Seminole farmer prepares to go into his fields.

Farming

Seminole farmers grow produce such as watermelons and tomatoes to brighten winter's dinner tables in the colder parts of the country. Citrus fruits are prime crops, and several thousand acres of Seminole-owned lemon and grapefruit groves border the road called "Alligator Alley," which crosses southern Florida.

Gaming and "The New Buffalo"

Many Floridians say that the Seminole bingo and casino games are "the new buffalo" because the money from these legal gambling operations have helped the tribe to prosper. Indeed, careful investment of gaming profits has brought income to the Seminoles. At the same time, however, the whole economy of the state of Florida has benefited from all Seminole business enterprises.

Languages

Most of the Seminoles today are **bilingual.** Along with English, many also speak Miccosukee (Mikasuki or Hitchiti), and others speak Muskogee, especially the Cow Creek Seminoles and most Oklahoma Seminoles. While the Miccosukee and Muskogee languages are related, one is not understood by speakers of the other.

Many place names that dot our modern maps of Florida give us fascinating hints about the Seminole past: Tallahassee (old town), Loxahatchee (terrapin river), Okeechobee (big water), Chattahoochee (red rocks), and Apopka (potato-eating place). We use native words each time we mention Miami, Pensacola, or the gentle, endangered manatee.

The living presence of Seminoles and their ancestors continues to be with us in many ways. Seminole foods and medicines enhance our modern lives. Seminole endurance reminds us of the great strength of native traditions.

Seminole young people are studying to be tomorrow's leaders. Many of their parents are lawyers, administrators, artists, singers and musicians, nurses and midwives, seamstresses and designers, teachers, pilots, cowboys, and corporate directors. The wisdom of their elders lives as a proud tradition with a bright, promising future.

Chief James E. Billie, leader of the Seminole Nation, is also a singer of pop, rock, and western music, a poet and a helicopter pilot.

How to Make a Seminole Smoothie

Here is a delicious Florida citrus drink that you can make. It is very much like the ones that the Seminole people serve at their gatherings, particularly at rodeos and powwows. A Seminole smoothie is both refreshing and easy to make—plus it satisfies your thirst and is good for you.

You will need:

1 fresh, ripe orange, cut in half, seeds removed
1 fresh lemon, cut in half, seeds removed
4 ounces of water, plus 8 ice cubes
2 8-ounce glasses (filled with this ice)
4 tablespoons of sugar, or honey (more or less)
1 16-ounce measuring cup
2 slices of fresh orange to trim tops of glasses

Yummy smoothies.

Directions:

1. Squeeze the juice from the citrus fruits into the large measuring cup.

2. Add the sugar and water. Stir well until blended together.

3. Pour over the ice in the two glasses. Distribute evenly.

4. Top the rim of each glass with a fresh orange slice. Or you might use a fresh-cut strawberry, some grapes, or cherries.

5. Serve, and enjoy!

Seminole Greeting

from Chief James E. Billie

Che-hun-tamo,	How are you?
He-ma-ne-ta-ke	It is good to gather
He-thou-sha!	Again!
Ha-shou-bou-sho-co-wa.	I hope the sun will be shining.
Sho-naa-bish.	Thank you.

Chief James E. Billie has been elected to six terms in office and leads his tribe toward the 21st century with confidence. A handsome figure in his colorful Seminole jacket and scarf, he is a popular singer, poet, and pop-rock-western musician with his own band. Chief Billie is also a Vietnam veteran and pilots his own helicopter to tribal locations and ranching operations around Florida.

Chief James E. Billie leads his tribe proudly and confidently into the 21st century.

41

Seminole Chronology

10,000– 11,000 years ago	Prehistoric Indians live in southeastern North America.
1513	Ponce de León names the land "Florida."
1565	Spanish settlers establish St. Augustine, Florida.
1607	English settle at Jamestown, Virginia.
1715	Yamassee Indians rise up against English settlers in the southern Carolinas.
1763	Spain transfers control of Florida to Great Britain.
1774–1781	American colonies win independence from Great Britain.
1783	Treaty of Paris returns Florida to Spanish rule.
1789	United States Constitution is adopted.
1817	The United States and the Seminoles fight First Seminole War.
1821	Spain transfers Florida to the United States.
1830	Indian Removal Act is passed, mandating removal of eastern Indian tribes.
1835–1842	Second Seminole War with the United States.
1837	U.S. troops capture Seminole warriors under a flag of truce.
1868	Seminole Nation and capital are established in Wewoka, Oklahoma.
1902	Drilling for oil and natural gas begins in Oklahoma.
1911	Big Cypress and Dania reservations are created for Florida Seminoles.
1923	The Greater Seminole Oil Field opens near Wewoka, Oklahoma.
1935	The Brighton Reservation is established for Florida Seminoles.
1947	The Everglades are named a national park and wildlife preserve.
1957	Seminole Tribe of Florida establishes its own constitution.
1961	Miccosukee Tribe of Florida is established.

1963	The first Seminole newspaper, *Smoke Signals*, is established. Later, it is called the *Seminole Tribune*.
1967	Betty Mae Jumper is the first woman elected to chair any tribe in North America in the 20th Century.
1968	Oath of Unity is signed by Choctaw, Cherokee, Seminole, and Miccosukee tribes, establishing United South and Eastern tribes (USET).
1990	The *Seminole Tribune* receives the Robert F. Kennedy Journalism Award from Ethel Kennedy.
1992	Seminoles in Florida and Oklahoma collect land claims against the United States for land lost through broken treaties.
1996	The Fort Pierce reservation is established in Florida, joining Tampa, Immokalee, Big Cypress, Hollywood (Dania), and Brighton reservations.
1996	The Seminole Tribe of Florida's budget exceeds $100 million.

Glossary

Ancestors Distant relatives who lived long ago.

Archaeology The careful recovery and study of remains of the way humans lived in the past.

Astringent A substance that draws together soft living tissue. Often used to stop minor bleeding.

Auction The sale of goods to the highest bidder.

Bilingual Speaking two languages.

Black boards Boards used to shape hair styles. Not used much today.

Bureau of Indian Affairs (BIA) An agency established by the U.S. government in 1824 to oversee Indian tribes and reservations.

Chickee An open-sided, thatched-roof home.

Clan People who are related to each other within a tribe.

Egret A type of heron that has long plumes, or feathers.

Elder A respected older person.

Everglades A broad area of marshlands, swamp, and forest in south-central Florida.

Green Corn Ceremony An annual event of thanksgiving, renewal, and purification, which includes special dances, foods, and prayers.

Guerrilla A type of warfare characterized by sudden raids and ambushes.

Herb A plant whose leaves, stems, seeds, or roots are used for medicine, for flavor in cooking, or for fragrance.

Hypertension High blood pressure.

Lease A method of renting out land usually over an agreed period of time.

Manatee A tropical, plant-eating mammal that lives in calm, coastal waters. It is gray and fishlike in shape but with a flattened paddle on its hind end. It has fleshy lips with bristles. Manatees are protected by law in Florida.

Mixed-blood The child of a marriage of Indian and white or black parents.

Patchwork Colorful pieces of cloth carefully sewn together in fine designs making special patterns.

Peninsula A body of land almost surrounded by water, yet connected to the mainland. The state of Florida is a peninsula.

Powwow An Indian social gathering often lasting days over a weekend, and including dancing, drumming, foods, and crafts.

Regal Dignified, as a king or queen.

Reservations Special lands set aside for Indians by the U.S. government.

Rickrack Narrow, zigzag braid or ribbon used as trimming on clothing or household linens.

Savannas A tropical or subtropical grassland that contains scattered trees and undergrowth that can survive during drought.

Semitropical Region bordering on the tropical zone. It is sometimes called subtropical.

Shaman A person who acts as an intermediary between the natural and supernatural worlds to cure illness, predict the future, and direct spiritual forces.

Subsidize To aid or promote something with public funds.

Traditions A group's most honored beliefs and practices carried forward from past generations.

Resources

Further Reading

Estep, Irene. *Seminoles.* McLemont, 1963.

Garbarino, Merwyn S. *The Seminole.* Philadelphia, PA: Chelsea House, 1989.

Hall, Gordon. *Osceola.* New York: Holt, Rinehart & Winston, 1964.

Jumper, Betty Mae. *Legends of the Seminoles.* Sarasota, FL: Pineapple Press, 1994. Illustrated by Guy LaBree, with a Foreword by Chief James E. Billie.

Koslow, Phillip. *The Seminole Indians.* Philadelphia, PA: Chelsea House Junior Library, 1994.

Oppenheim, Joanne. *Osceola, Seminole Warrior.* Mahwah, NJ: Troll Associates, 1979.

Seminole Tribune, the "Voice of the Unconquered." Published bimonthly at 6300 Stirling Road, Hollywood, FL 33024 (954) 967-3416.

Viola, Herman J. *North American Indians: An Introduction to the Lives of America's Native Peoples, from the Inuit of the Arctic to the Zuni of the Southwest.* Crown Publishers, 1996.

Viola, Herman J. *Osceola.* (American Indian Series) Austin, TX: Raintree Steck-Vaughn, 1993, 1996 (paper).

Audiovisuals

"The Seminole Tribe of Florida: On the Path of Self-Reliance," narrated by Chief James Billie. This 30-minute video interviews many tribal members and discusses their progress.

Website

The Seminole Tribe's address on the Worldwide Web is: www.seminoletribe.com

Places to Visit

The Seminole Tribe of Florida   [corporate offices]
6300 Stirling Road
Hollywood, FL 33024   (954) 967-3416

Ah-Tah-Thi-Ki Museum *"...a place to learn...a place to remember"*
Big Cypress Reservation
HC-61, Box 21A   [17 miles north of Alligator Alley, I-75]
Clewiston, FL 33440   (954) 792-0745

Anhinga Indian Museum & Art Gallery
5791 S. State Road 7
Ft. Lauderdale, FL 33314   (954) 581-0416

The Native Village & Native American Gift Shop
3551 N. State Road 7   (US 441) [educational programs
Hollywood, FL 33024   & live animals]
                                         (954) 961-4519

Miccosukee Indian Village & Airboat Tours & Restaurant
P.O. Box 440021   [located 25 miles west of Miami, US 41]
Miami, FL 33144   (305) 223-8380

Big Cypress Campground
Big Cypress Indian Reservation   (800) 437-4103

Seminole Nation Museum
6th St & Muskogee Ave.
Wewoka, OK 74884   (405) 257-5485

Seminole Nation Tribal Complex
US Hwy 270   (405) 257-6287
Wewoka, OK 74884

The Five Civilized Tribes Museum & Trading Post
Agency Hill, Honor Heights Drive
Muskogee, OK 74401   (918) 683-1701

Index

Numbers in italics indicate illustration or map.